MW00614649

Snow in a Silver Bowl

A Quest for the World of *Yūgen*

Hiroaki Sato

Snow in a Silver Bowl:
A Quest for the World of *Yūgen*

ISBN 978-1-936848-23-2

Red Moon Press
PO Box 2461
Winchester VA
22604-1661 USA
www.redmoonpress.com

Second Revised Edition

Cover design by MC Project based on
Masaaki Noda's sculpture, "Awakening."

Dedicated to
Abe Hinako, Ishii Tatsuhiko,
& Nancy Rossiter

Contents

Notes & Acknowledgments

All Japanese names are given the Japanese way, family name first. Unless noted, all translations are mine.

•••••

I thank Juna Amano for her photograph, "Heart of the Shadow"; Hashi no Kai (Bridge Society) for Yoshikoshi Ken's photograph of Kanze Hisao dancing in *Nonomiya*; Christiane Krömer for her linoleum cut, "Alligators and Turtles"; Masaaki Noda for his painting, "Once"; Bruce Schwarz for the photograph of Isamu Noguchi's "Water Stone" at the Metropolitan Museum of Art; Geoff van Kirk for his photograph of the Rakushisha, in Saga, Kyoto.

•••••

The Rakushisha, "The Hut Where Persimmons Drop," was the Kyoto hermitage of the *haikai* poet Mukai Kyorai (1651–1704). Matsuo Bashō (1644–94) visited it on the 24th of Twelfth Month 1689 and stayed there from the 18th of Fourth Month to the 4th of Fifth Month 1691 and wrote

The Saga Diary. He also visited the hut on the 22nd of the intercalary Fifth Month 1694 and wrote a *kasen*, a 36-link renga, with Kyorai and four others. The *kasen* is known by the first word of Bashō's *hokku*, *Yanagikori* (*Willow Case*).

•••••

I thank Abe Hinako for sending me books, Ishii Tatsuhiko for answering a host of questions, Nancy Rossiter and the late Robert Fagan for editing the manuscript.

Hiroaki Sato

Snow in a Silver Bowl

A Quest for the World of *Yūgen*

Yūgen 幽玄—*yū* pronounced like "you" as in "you and I" and the *g* of *gen* with a hard *g* as in "geisha"—is an important Japanese aesthetic concept that may date from the days when Japanese tried to digest the early onslaught of Chinese culture, in the sixth and seventh centuries. It is so important, nay, so unique to Japanese culture, indeed, that *foreigners* can never fathom its profundity, many Japanese love to think. In that regard, yūgen is like the two other Japanese aesthetic concepts, which are in truth its descendents, *wabi* わび and *sabi* さび.

But can't they?

I ask Doris Bargen what yūgen evokes for her. Ms. Bargen, a German scholar of Stanley Elkin who turned to classical Japanese literature when she read *The Tale of Genji*, responds by mentioning "a cortège"—in a PBS documentary on Eleanor Roosevelt:

 . . . there is the funeral scene of President Roosevelt, with his coffin on an old rattling

3

cart drawn by horses, and then the horse without a rider next to the coffin. And the silence, with only the unadorned sounds of this cortège.

The Tale of Genji, written in the early eleventh century by a court lady known as Murasaki Shikibu, is a "vast chronicle of court life . . . regarded unreservedly as the greatest single work in Japanese literature," to quote William Rose Benét's *Reader's Encyclopedia* (1965). The novel's influence on Japanese literature, drama, and art in subsequent centuries has been pervasive, to put it mildly.

Leza Lowitz, an American poet who now teaches yoga in Tokyo, thought of a different cortège, from a different perspective: "John Kennedy, Jr., saluting his father's casket at the funeral," and added:

> . . . I also think of a portrait of Greta Garbo's face, in black and white, with her hair pulled back, eyes sad and mysterious. To me, her face and persona, cast in shadow, exude a quality of quiet grace and mystery. Much is left unsaid. More is evoked than invoked.

Perhaps that is the essence of yūgen. Like the mist covering the mountains at dawn.

Asked the same question, Liza Dalby, begins by saying, "Hint: Not a woman," "The '*kū*' of '*shiki soku ze kū*'" (of which we will see more later), and cites, as an image embodying yūgen, "A well-pruned persimmon tree." Ms. Dalby, "the American geisha," has written, among others, *The Tale of Murasaki* (2000), the fictitious autobiography of the author of *The Tale of Genji*.

Persimmons have gained popularity in the United States in the past decade or so, at least on the East Coast, but may still not be familiar to most Americans. So I ask her for more images, and a few days later she reports:

Your [query] gave me strange dreams of yūgen last night. Somehow most of the images that appeared were musical—Beethoven's late string quartets and Mozart's "Requiem." And then there was the stone cathedral in Avila, Spain.

Rakushisha 落柿舎
"The Hut Where Persimmons Drop"
Saga, Kyoto
Photograph by Geoff van Kirk
(See Acknowledgment Page)

My teacher of poetry, Lindley Williams Hubbell (1901–94), if asked what embodied yūgen for him, would certainly have agreed with her about Beethoven's last quartets. He often cited them, along with the final self-portraits of Rembrandt, as exemplars of art in which "form and content have become fused in a unique personal expression," as he put it in *Lectures on Shakespeare* (1962).

But being a Shakespearean scholar, he naturally included some of the Bard's plays as achieving that state of "the ultimate refinement of technique" as well—those in the "third, final period" of his work. Among them are, he said, *Hamlet*, *King Lear*, and *The Tempest*. As to an example in English poetry in which "technique and content become one, being fused in the creative imagination," he gave this, from *Macbeth* (III, ii):

After life's fitful fever he sleeps well.

Rand Castile, an admirer of Mr. Hubbell's poetry and the author of *The Way of Tea* (1971), would also choose Beethoven's string quartets. But he is likely to be in particular accord with Ms. Dalby in her dreaming of the stone cathedral in Avila, Spain. Mr. Castile, who led the way in exhibiting Japanese art in the last three decades of the twentieth century in the United States, has listed a number of things as incarnating the aesthetic notion of yūgen, among them "Louis Khan's Kimbell Art Museum, Andō Tadao's 'Church of Light' (west of Kyoto), and one of his houses in Kobe." Andō Tadao, a self-taught architect, designed the site for Japan Flora 2000, a "flower fair" on Awaji Island. The site had 750 species of flowers, with a total of 390,000 bulbs, planted in it.

Let us look at some of the other things Mr. Castile cited:

— the paintings of Morris Graves, Ad Reinhardt, early (pin-stripe) Frank Stella, some of the more abstract Turners;
— Bergman's *Seventh Seal* and Fellini's *La Strada*, some of Kurosawa's [movies], and Ishioka Eiko's set for the "Golden Pavilion" scene in the film *Mishima*;

—the best of *sō-hitta-shibori kosode* 総匹田絞
小袖 and some *obi*;

He also listed a number of poems, lines
from poems, and prose passages, beginning
with Sappho:

The moon and the Pleiades
Have set. It is midnight.
The hours pass.
I lie alone.
　　　　　　—*tr. Lindley Williams Hubbell*

and a line from Shakespeare's "Sonnet 33":

Gilding pale streams with heavenly alchemy…

which Mr. Castile calls "the perfect English
utterance," and ending his impromptu cata-
logue with a passage from Guy de Maupasant's
Boule de Suif:

… A curtain of glistening snow-flakes
descended toward the earth, veiling every
human form and covering inanimate objects
with an icy fleece. In the intense stillness

of the town, plunged in the deep repose of winter, no sound was audible save the vague, indefinable, fluttering whisper of the falling snow, felt rather than heard, the mingling of airy atoms, which seemed to fill all space and envelop the whole world.

—*tr. Marjorie Laurie*

So what is yūgen?

Doris Bargen adds to the image of a Presidential cortège a scholarly reference. She finds a book by Werner Sollors called *Amiri Baraka/LeRoi Jones: The Quest for a "Populist Modernism"* (1978). It says on page 3, she reports, that in 1958 Amiri Baraka/LeRoi Jones and Hettie Roberta Cohen "got married in a Buddhist temple on New York's Upper West Side" and "coedited the avant-garde literary magazine *Yugen* (meaning 'elegance, beauty, grace, transcendence of these things, and also nothing at all')."

So I ask my wife, Nancy, to check the matter at the New York Public Library where Mr. Hubbell worked in the map room for years and, sure enough, she finds the magazine *Yūgen*—yes, with the macron for *u* and, yes, carrying, in its first issue, the definition: "YŪGEN means elegance, beauty, grace, transcendence of these things, and also nothing at all." The calligraphy used for the cover, by Rachel Spitzer, appears to be an attempt to reproduce the Chinese character 憂 (hesitant, depressing), not 幽 of 幽玄, though, as it happens, both characters are pronounced the same, as often does not happen, in Chinese and in Japanese bastardization. But what's eye-opening is the knowing acuity of the last part of the definition: "transcendence of these things, and also nothing at all."

Even more fascinating, in the second issue of the slim magazine, proclaimed to be "a new consciousness in arts and letters," the definition given is different but as striking: "the flower of the miraculous." In the fourth issue, what is given in lieu of a definition is an apparent Zen parable:

Aruna (the nun) had been in a cave meditating twenty years. On the day she came out she met two monks on the road. One looked at her legs, the other gave a wolf whistle.

Who was behind all this casual erudition? Gary Snyder, who is among the contributors to the second issue and was studying Zen, in Kyoto, at the time? Or his scholarly friends in Japan, such as Burton Watson and Phillip Yampolsky, who went on to become Columbia professors? Both Watson and Yampolsky are among those who wrote tributes in *Gary Snyder: Dimensions of a Life* (1991).

It's about time to look at yūgen in Japanese tradition.

If you take a poll in Japan as to which artistic form the word *yūgen* brings to mind, the majority will say, "nō drama." This, in an important way, is correct. But there is an apparent contradiction in the response, because, if you go on to ask for a definition of the word, most Japanese are likely to say it suggests something "dark," "mysterious," "ambiguous" or, as my tanka poet friend Ishii Tatsuhiko put it, "artistically contrived ambiguity." It may also suggest something "ancient," even "withered." Ōba Takemitsu, Starr Conservator of Asian Art at the Metropolitan Museum of Art, asked over a drink to define yūgen, came up with the image of "an old man emerging out of mist."

Yet the most conspicuous aspects of the nō paraphernalia, the costumes, are often resplendently gorgeous to the point of gaudiness. As Ernest Francisco Fenollosa, whose nō translations Ezra Pound turned into poetry, for one, described them, they "are very rich, of splendid gold brocades and soft floss-silk weaving, or of Chinese tapestry stitch, and are very costly." In fact, the nō stage itself, with its highly polished floor, gives the impression of bright-lit clarity—unless you go to an old nō theater of a declining troupe.

If this is a contradiction, where does it come from?

As scholars have it, there are three sources for yūgen: Taoism, Japanese court poetry, and the greatest proponent of nō drama, Zeami Motokiyo (c1364–1443).

The origins of the term yūgen are usually traced to Taoism. *Lao-tzu* (*Lao-zi*), which is thought to predate *Chuang-tzu* (*Zhuang-zi*) by about a century, famously begins:

> The Way that can be called "the Way" is not the constant Way.
> The name that can be called "the name" is not the constant name.
> Nameless was the beginning of Heaven and Earth.
> Named was the mother of all things.
> Therefore we can see subtlety in constant nothingness,
> we can see complexity in constant beingness.
> These two come out of the same thing but have different names.
> That same thing we say is ineffable.
> Ineffable, yes, ineffable, it is the gate to all subtleties.

Famously begins, I said, but this passage is regarded as among the most abstruse to comprehend in *Lao-tzu,* also known as *Tao-*

tē-ching (*Dao-de-jing*). Herbert A. Giles, the British Sinologist who proudly noted that his *History of Chinese Literature* (1901) was "the first [such] attempt made in any language, including Chinese," regarded *Lao-tzu* as "a collection of many genuine utterances of Lao Tzu, sandwiched however between thick wads of padding from which little meaning can be extracted except by enthusiasts who curiously enough disagree absolutely among themselves."

Fortunately, among the genuine utterances—according to Giles at any rate—is the first line in the paragraph quoted above. But even here, readings and translations vary. Giles interpreted it to mean "The Way (Tao) which can be walked upon is not the eternal Way." In *The Way and Its Power* (1938), Arthur Waley took it to mean "The Way that can be told of is not an unvarying Way." In his massive *Source Book in Chinese Philosophy* (1963), Wing-tsit Chan followed Waley somewhat and put it: "The Tao (Way) that can be told of is not the eternal Tao." And so on.

What concerns us here, though, is the word I've given as "ineffable": 玄, the second of the two ideographs that make up yūgen, 幽玄, for it is thought to mean the same thing as the two-character word. What is 玄 (*xuan* in Chinese)?

Waley gave it as "the Mystery" (and, in the next line where the ideograph is repeated for emphasis, "Darker than any Mystery"). Chan, on the other hand, interpreted it to mean "deep and profound" (and, in the next line, "deeper and more profound"), although when he gave *Lao Tzu* a separate monograph (1979), he apparently decided that Waley's choice was preferable; this time he rendered the word, albeit without the definite article and the capitalization, as "mystery" (and, in the next line, as "mystery and more mystery"). Does this clarify the matter?

Ezra Pound while working on Fenollosa's English drafts of *kanshi*, poems written in classical Chinese, famously committed the misunderstanding that all Chinese characters were pictographs. Chinese never made that mistake. As early as the year 100, Xu Shen (58?–147?), in compiling the dictionary of Chinese ideographs *Shuowen* (説文), divided all known ideographs into six categories, only one of them to those thought to represent actual objects. He put 玄 in that category, and provided it with the following explication:

玄幽遠也。象幽。
玄 means "faint and remote."
It is also written 幽.

Here we already have the two characters for *yūgen*, 幽 and 玄, and the suggestion is made that these are interchangeable.

Etymologically, the Japanese Sinologist and lexicographer Todō Akiyasu (1915–1985) tells us, the ideograph 玄 can be separated into two parts: the bottom, 幺, which suggests "a thin thread," and the top, 一, which represents a line, with the wiggle sticking out from it indicating the upper end of the thread. The result 玄 means "hardly visible."

As for 幽, it consists of two thin threads placed side by side and the ideograph 山,

"mountain." Two thin threads buried in a mountain are hard to make out, so the ideograph means "dark and hard to distinguish," Tōdō tells us.

For his part, Xu Shen had added to his explanation of 玄 the observation 黑而有赤色者為玄, "That which is black with a tinge of red forms 玄." As a result, the ideograph 玄 has been strongly associated with darkness or black, says another Japanese lexicographer of Chinese ideographs, Shirakawa Shizuka (1910–2006).

At any rate, the opening paragraph of *Lao-tzu* may deter some readers as being too ancient, alien, and abstruse, so I should note that for many decades now there has been debate among Western explicators of Taoism on whether "logos" or even "God" might not be right for "the Way (Tao)." And because The Gospel According to St. John states, "In the beginning was the Word, and the Word was with God, and the Word was God," some have argued that Taoism, sometimes called "the philosophy of 玄," represents the antithesis of

Christian thought. One scholar, Herrlee Creel, has also pointed out, in *What Is Taoism? And Other Studies in Chinese Cultural History* (1970), that Plato and Lao-tzu start out with the same premise and reach opposite conclusions.

To get closer to "the mystery" of 玄, let us look at the next section of *Lao-tzu* that employs the character. Section 6 says, in its entirety:

> The valley deity never dies.
> It is called the ineffable female.
> The gate of the ineffable female
> is called the root of Heaven and Earth.
> It is ever continuous
> and even in use never tires.

The "valley" and "gate" here are, we're told, both metaphors for the vulva—or, in Freudian parlance, the womb, perhaps. Because of this, the passage brings to my mind a poem by Lindley Williams Hubbell:

Willendorf Venus

The Venus of Willendorf

Breast mountains, buttock mountains,
Pubescence like the grass that covers the
    prairies,
You are warmth, you are comfort,
You are earth in the season when the sun
    grows hot again.
You are the first goddess
And the last.
Fertility outlives invention.
The arts have issued from your great belly.

All cycles are contained in you.
You are plowed long before the earth is
    plowed.
You receive the plunging male
With a yell of triumph.

Blending with Nature
& Delicate Sentiments

The dating of *Lao-tzu* is said to be problematic, but in time the term combining the two characters 幽 and 玄, with the first added to the second for balance," we're told, began to be used to mean profundity, subtlety, or, sometimes, poesy. And as Chinese books and concepts began to pour into Japan, six to eight hundred years after the formation of *Lao-tzu*, the term *yūgen* (in Japanese pronunciation of course) began to be employed by Japanese poets, in the end acquiring a distinct sense. Or senses.

The first one to line up sets of poems to illustrate yūgen was Mibu no Tadamine, of the tenth century, in his treatise on poetics, compiled in 945, *Jittei* (*Ten Styles*), although some doubt the attribution. Here are the first three from one set of five, all written in the tanka form.

Singing of the snow falling

冬ながら空より花の散り来るは雪のあなたは春にやあ
るらむ

Though winter, from the sky blossoms flutter
down; beyond the clouds it must be spring
—*Kiyohara no Fukayabu*

*For the screen of North Princess's coming-of-age
ceremony*

行きやらで山路くらしつ時鳥いま一声の聞かまほしさに

Unable to go further I spent all day on mountain
paths, yearning to hear a cuckoo's single call
just once more
—*Minamoto no Kintada*

*On someone on a mountain path for the Vestal's
screen*

散り散らず聞かまほしきを故郷の花見てかへる人もあ
わなむ

Fallen not fallen I'd like to ask: would one were
who saw blossoms in Old Town, returning
—*Ise*

24

The first poem is based on a conceit known as *mitate*, the art of deliberately mistaking one thing for another—in this instance, snowflakes for cherry blossoms. The second and third were composed to match screen paintings, a prevalent practice at the time. In the headnote to the second, the North Princess is Princess Kōshi (920–57), the fourteenth daughter of Emperor Daigo (885–930). Her coming-of-age ceremony was held in the Eighth Month of 933. Poetics dictated that the *hototogisu* (the lesser or Asian cuckoo, different from the common cuckoo), the harbinger of summer, be awaited for its rare, single call, though in real life its calls seem never to be singles, but consecutive.

In the headnote to the third poem, the Vestal may be Princess Kyōshi (902–15), Emperor Daigo's fourth daughter, who was selected to be Vestal when she was two years old. A vestal, or *saiin*, is a virgin princess appointed to be the high priestess of the Kamo Shrines, Upper and Lower. In the poem, the Old Town is Nara, Japan's capital until 794. The blossoms mentioned are cherry blossoms, the most prized poetic embodiment of spring. Ise, who wrote this poem, served Emperor Uda (867–931). Later she was Prince Atsuyoshi's lover. She bore a child to each.

These poems "enter the state of yūgen," Tadamine judged, because they describe "elevated" yearnings to blend with nature. The "nature" aspect of yūgen will remain important. The nō drama actor-writer-theorist Zeami, for one, would go on to posit that theater is *hana*, "flower."

But Tadamine did not confine himself to yearnings for nature in defining yūgen in poetry. He also selected a set of five poems from the category of love, which is as important as the categories of the four seasons in the classical poetic canon, and described them as "ineffable, yes, ineffable." Here are four of them.

Untitled

たのめつゝ来ぬ夜あまたになりぬれば待たじと思ふぞ
　待つにまされる

Nights he promised to come but did not accumu-
lating, deciding not to wait is better than
waiting

—*Kakinomoto no Hitomaro*

After I was exiled, I sent word

君が住む宿の梢を行くゆくとかくるゝまでにかへり見し
　はや

The treetops of the house you live in I turned
to see until I went farther and they were
hidden

—*Honorary Prime Minister*

*In the Eighth Month of the seventeenth year of Engi,
I made a poem according to an imperial edict*

来ぬ人を下に待ちつゝ久方の月をあはれといはぬ夜ぞ
　なき

Waiting secretly for someone who never comes
there's no night I do not say, "The eternal
moon's beautiful"

—*Ki no Tsurayuki*

Untitled

思ひつゝぬればや人の見へつらむ夢と知りせばさめざ
　らましを

Because, thinking of him, I fell asleep I saw him;
　had I known it was a dream I would not have
　awakened

　　　　　　　　　　　　　　—Ono no Komachi

These poems describe sentiments that
are "difficult to reveal" and "difficult to
express." The first one, attributed to Hitomaro, is a sigh of remonstration. A lover,
despite his promises, fails to come to visit
for many a night, so the speaker—here the
poet is likely to be speaking in a woman's
voice—tells herself that "deciding not to
wait is better than waiting." Hitomaro is the
greatest among the earlier poets in Japan's
oldest extant anthology *Man'yōshū* (*Collection
of Ten Thousand Leaves*), revered by the ninth
century as a "poetic sage."

The second poem describes the pain
of separation in a muted, indirect way.
The scholar-poet Sugawara no Michizane
(845–903), here identified as "Honorary

28

Prime Minister," wrote it for his wife as he was being removed from Kyoto. He fell victim to slander when he was Minister of the Right and was exiled to Dazaifu, a remote outpost in Kyushu. "Honorary Prime Minister" is his posthumous title. After his death, a series of disasters struck Kyoto, among them the untimely death of the ranking courtier who had maligned him. People said his vengeful soul was the cause. So, to pacify him, the imperial court presented him with higher ranks: Minister of the Left, in 923, and Prime Minister, in 993.

The third poem, also written in a woman's role, again has to do with someone trying to deal with her lover who continues to disappoint her by failing to keep his promise. People ask her why she's been staying up of late. Unable to say she's been waiting for her fickle lover, she says it's because she cannot miss the beautiful moon. By the lunar calendar, Eighth Month is the last month of autumn. The moon on the fifteenth of that month—by the solar calendar around the end of September—is regarded as the most beautiful. So the speaker of the poem has a good excuse to stay up late. The moon also takes pride of place among poetic topics of autumn. Ki no Tsurayuki, who wrote this poem, was, like Mibu no Tadamine, an editor of the first imperial anthology of Japanese verse *Kokinwakashū* (*Collection of Poems Ancient and Modern*).

The fourth poem is a sigh-like lament of someone living in a world where dream and reality cannot be separated. It is based on at least two conceits. One says the state of being in love should not be made public (as is intimated by the preceding poem), let alone divulged to the person you are in love with, that the consequent pain of it must be quietly endured. The other is the notion that, if you are unable to meet and make love to someone you love, you may be able to do so in dreams by thinking about him constantly. This poem, along with two others by the same poet, Ono no Komachi, opens the "Love Poems: II" section of the *Kokinwakashū*.

Komachi is associated with the semi-mythological beauty Sotōri because the introduction to the *Kokinwakashū* mentioned the two in the same breath. As the *Nihon shoki* (*History of Japan*), compiled in 720, has it, the name Sotōri comes from the fact that "she was so beautiful her glow shone through her robe," which is exactly what her name means. The association helped turn Komachi into an exceptional beauty herself and made, at some point in history, the name Komachi synonymous with "a beautiful woman."

The notions suggested by Tadamine in the two sets of poems to illustrate yūgen as "ineffable, yes, ineffable" would be refined and elaborated in the centuries to come. But two basic ingredients would remain: the emphasis on nature or the luminous side of it, conveyed with overtones, and the emphasis on regrets, disappointment, or frustrations, described with restraint and sadness.

The introduction to the *Kokinwakashū* noted that in her poetry Ono no Komachi suggested "a noblewoman suffering from some ailment." This image adumbrated the one the poet Kamo no Chōmei (?1155–1216) set down as given by his teacher of poetry, Monk Shun'e (1113–95?), to visualize the aesthetic notion of yūgen. In his treatise on poetics *Mumyōshō* (*Nameless Jottings*), Chōmei recollected, in Socratic dialogue, how the renowned poet tried to define it:

> Someone asked: . . . . When it comes to the yūgen that you've just mentioned, I find it hard to grasp what it should be like. I'd be grateful to learn what it is.
>
> Someone said in reply: How a poem works is altogether hard to grasp. . . . Above all, the matter of yūgen confuses you the moment you hear the word. . . . But those who have attained the state tell us that, in essence, it simply has to be an overtone that doesn't manifest itself in words, a feeling that isn't visible in the way the poem is made.

When the sentiment is deeply felt and the words are extremely delicate, these virtues come into being by themselves.

For example, the way the evening sky appears in autumn, it has neither color nor voice. Still, though you cannot tell wherefrom and wherefore, tears well up and never cease. Those with no heart think nothing of this, loving as they do only [cherry] blossoms and maple leaves.

Or it is as if you have a passing glimpse of a noblewoman who, though apparently she has some resentment, does not express it in words but hides it deeply in her heart, and you say to yourself, "Ah," and you feel more pain, feel greater pity than you might when you see someone airing her complaints, using all the words she knows, wringing her sleeves.

There was also, one must not fail to note, the image Li Bai (Li Po: 701–62) drew in one of a series of poems on neglected women. In the quatrain "Resentment," China's "poetic immortal" (*shixian*) spoke of a beauty (*meiren*):

The beauty, her pearly curtain raised,
sits deep inside, her willowy eyebrows knit;

only the moist traces of tears visible,
whom she resents in her heart no one can tell.

Seven hundred years later, the court lady Monk Shun'e envisaged would strike a chord in modernist Ecuadorian poetry that was much influenced by Poe, Samain, Verlaine, and Baudelaire. Jorge Carrera Andrade tells us, in *Reflections on Spanish American Poetry*, that Ernesto Noboa y Caamaño (1891–1927) and some of his fellow poets "considered bodily ailment as 'exquisite ills' conducive to esthetic refinement and death as the supreme grace conceded to mankind." Caamaño, for example, wrote *"En la tarde de Sol"* ("On an Afternoon of Sun") with the following lines:

*Enferma de belleza, de ensueño y de elegancia,
huellas la blanca arena con paso distraído
dejando una áurea estela de espiritual fragancia*

Sick of beauty, daydream, and elegance,
you mark the white sand with your distracted steps
leaving behind a golden trail of spiritual
  fragrance.

       —*tr. Forrest Gander*

Princess Shikishi, Chōmei's contemporary though she died much earlier than he, in 1201, has left us a poem which could easily have been composed to embody Shun'e's and, later, Caamaño's idea of a noble or graceful woman suffering. The topic on which she wrote the poem was "love to be endured." "String of beads" is a metaphor for "life."

玉の緒よ絶えなばたえねながらへばしのぶることのよは
　　りもぞする

String of beads, if you must break, break; if you
　　last longer, my endurance is sure to weaken

Fujiwara no Teika (1162–1241) chose this poem to present the princess in his minianthology, *Hyakunin isshu* (*One Hundred Poems by One Hundred Poets*), which went on to become a canonical text. Among the later poets who admired Shikishi's poetry, Shōtetsu (1381–1459), considered the following poems of hers as embodiments of yūgen:

Princess Shikishi
as imagined by Kanō Tan'yū (1602-74)

生きてよもあすまで人もつらからじこの夕暮をとはば問へかし

I wouldn't live and he wouldn't be this cruel till
   tomorrow; visit this evening if you ever do

忘れてはうち嘆かるゝゆふべかなわれのみ知りてすぐる月日を

Forgetful I grieve this evening, the months and
   days I've passed, I alone knowing

With the first of these two, Shōtetsu
noted what makes it engender yūgen is that
despite the imperative mood that makes up its
latter half, the poet is "not speaking to anyone,"
but she is "alone . . . in grief."

In this, Electra, of Sophocles, ranting,
cursing, spitting, has to be an aphelion of
yūgen. Yūgen is Ophelia when she sings in
her madness—

   And will'a not come again?
   And will'a not come again?
    No, no, he is dead;
    Go to thy deathbed;
   He never will come again. . . .

or as she is described by Gertrude:

> There on the pendent boughs her crownet
>   weeds
> Clamb'ring to hang, an envious sliver broke,
> When down her weedy trophies and herself
> Fell in the weeping brook. Her clothes spread
>   wide,
> And mermaid-like awhile they bore her up
> Which time she chanted snatches of old
>   lauds,
> As one incapable of her own distress,
> Or like a creature native and indued
> Unto that element. But long it could not be
> Till that her garments, heavy with their
>   drink,
> Pulled the poor wretch from her melodious
>   lay
> To muddy death.

Monk Shun'e, whose own poetry Retired Emperor Gotoba (1180–1239) compared to "an iris five feet long splashed with water" in his treatise on poetry *Go-kuden* (*His Majesty's Oral Transmissions*), goes on to add other images to explain yūgen:

> Again, it's as if an infant, an adorable one of course, says something, lisping, which you really can't understand, and you are touched, you just love him, you think what he has to say is worth hearing. . . .
>
> Again, when you look at an autumn mountain through a rift in clouds, though what you see is vague, you yearn to see more, speculating endlessly in your mind how fascinating must be the way maple leaves spread themselves all over the place, which is far superior to when everything is sparklingly clear.

So, what types of poems did Shun'e regard as embodying yūgen? According to Chōmei, Shun'e compared "good poems in the worldly sense" to crocheting (*katamon*, "fabric made by tight weaving") and the very best poems to brocades (*ukimon*, "floating fabric designs"). Here are two examples of the latter he cited.

ほのぼのと明石の浦の朝霧に島隠れゆく舟をしぞ思ふ

Faintly through Akashi Cove's morning mists, hiding behind the isles goes a boat for which I long

月やあらぬ春は昔の春ならぬわが身ひとつはもとの身にして

Not the moon, the spring is not the spring of old, my body alone remaining the body that once was

The first of these two was initially cited in the *Kokinwakashū*, with its authorship attributed to Kakinomoto no Hitomaro. Not long afterward, Fujiwara no Kintō (966-1041), put it in the highest rank when he graded poems by the Buddhist hierarchical scheme of nine "stages."

Akashi, a port or cove on the Island Sea, puns with "lighten," "light," hence modified by the preceding adverbial phrase, "dimly,"

"Alligators and Turtles"
Linoleum cut by Christiane Krömer

"faintly," what not. In ancient days, it was also a marine checkpoint. It faces Awaji, the largest of the 3,000 islands, mostly islets, that dot the waters. Kintō's contemporary, Monk Nōin (b. 988), who started the tradition of poets struck by wanderlust, listed Akashi among the *uta-makura*, place names to be sung of. By then, another of Kintō's contemporaries, Lady Murasaki, may already have added some literary sentiments to the place, as we shall see.

The poem — the original poem — appears innocuous at first glance. But it turns out to have several mysteries. Is it talking about a small rowing boat or an oceangoing sailboat that plied the waters between Japan and China? Is the boat or ship heading toward Awaji or moving behind a series of tiny isles (assuming they existed)? For that matter, is Awaji the only island visible from Akashi? (Even on this geographical point, opinions, historically, differ.) What is the role of the mist at daybreak? Is it possible to follow the movement of a marine vessel in the obfuscating dawn mist? Is it the mist, rather than an island or islands, that "hides" the vessel, even though the original phrase, *shima-gakure yuku*, suggests that it is an island or islands that hide it?

Asked about such things, the tanka poet Ishii Tatsuhiko replied:

The mention of "morning mist" suggests, because of the set phrase *asagiri-gakure*, "morning-mist-hidden," that both the vessel and the island(s) are hazy at best or invisible. This, in turn, suggests that the poet, fully aware that the Inland Sea is famous for its countless isles, is imagining a boat or a ship moving through it. He may have seen a boat, but the rest is what he imagines.

This old poem, attributed to Hitomaro, is unlike a modern tanka in that it does not sing of definite time and space. Instead, the poet, seeing a boat leave the mist-enveloped cove of Akashi, thinks of a slow-moving temporal passage and a grand spatial movement as he imagines the boat moving from one isle to another.

Akashi had a checkpoint in ancient times. That meant that the area to the west of it was territory beyond the reach of the Capital. The boat not only will hide itself behind one isle after another, but it will in the end hide itself and disappear into the depths of alien territory, a different world.

The poem went on to become one of the *Kokinwakashū* pieces selected for "secret transmission"—poems only those in the know were supposed to be able to understand and whose true "meanings" were orally transmitted from one person to another—and the renga master Iio Sōgi (1421–1502), one of the privileged secret transmitters, did not forget to designate the poem as an exemplar of yūgen.

The second poem, "Not the moon," comes with a story in *Tales of Ise*, a collection of "poetic tales" that is thought to have taken its present shape by the end of the tenth century. The protagonist of many of the vignettes is Japan's Don Juan, Ariwara no Narihira (825–80), who is described in the *Sandai jitsuroku* (*True Records of Three Emperors*), the official history compiled in 901, as "quietly elegant, licentious and unconstrained, with no learning whatsoever, but good at poetry." The poem, "Not the moon," is preceded by the following tale:

> Once, when the Empress Dowager was living on Fifth Avenue, the East Side, a lady lived in the west-wing quarter [of the mansion]. A man deeply in love with her despite the circumstances used to visit her. But around the tenth of First Month she hid herself in some other place. He found out where she was, but it was not the sort of place someone like him could frequent, and he became even more depressed. In the First Month of the following year, when plum blossoms were in full bloom, he thought of what had happened in the previous year and visited the old place. But though he looked and looked, standing up, sitting down, nothing resembled what he had remembered. So, weeping, he lay on the barren wooden floor until the moon inclined and, thinking of the previous year, made this poem. . . .

The unnamed lady here is thought to be Fujiwara no Kōshi or Takaiko (842–910), the consort of Emperor Seiwa (850–81). Narihira was having an affair with the Empress.

Hugh Kenner tells us, in *The Pound Era* (1971), that Fenollosa extracted the following meaning from this poem through, no doubt, the interpretations his Japanese friends provided: "No moon! The spring is not the spring of old days—my person only is as it was and final body being (old)," and that Pound changed it to:

> No moon!
> The spring
> Is not the spring of the old days.
> My body
> Is not my body
> But only a body grown old.

The original poem, like Hitomaro's, has been subjected to a variety of interpretations, but admiration for it, as for Hitomaro's, has never wavered. Among Shun'e's contemporaries, Fujiwara no Shunzei (1114–1204), the supreme arbiter of poetry of the day, praised it as "infinitely felicitous."

Another poem Shun'e cited as an example of *ukimon*, "floating fabric designs"—this one by Minamoto no Toshiyori (1055–1129), famous for his comprehensive manual on poetics called *Zuinō* (*Essences*)—reads:

鶉鳴く真野の入江の浜風に尾花波寄る秋の夕暮
In the beach wind of Mano Inlet where quail call
　　pampas grass rolls in this autumn dusk

Retired Emperor Gotoba also thought highly of the poem, saying it was "beautiful." He then quoted Shunzei as observing, "A poem like this cannot be made easily." And that brings us to the poem Shunzei regarded as the greatest among his own compositions. As it happens, it, too, describes quail. And, as it happens, Shunzei was the first great promulgator of yūgen as a poetic criteria.

Shun'e tells the story.

Shun'e said, "When I was visiting the Lay Priest on Fifth Avenue, Third Rank [i.e., Shunzei], it occurred to me to ask him, 'Sir, among the poems you made yourself, which do you think is the best? People choose various poems, but I wouldn't want to use any of them. May I hear directly from you?' And he said,

夕されば野辺の秋風身にしみて鶉鳴くなり深草の里

Come evening moor's autumn wind chills my body and a quail calls in Deep Grass village

As far as I am concerned, this, I think, is something I'm very proud of.'"

"Deep Grass" is a translation of the place name Fukakusa, an area south of Kyoto, which at the time evidently was a semi-wild, sparsely populated grassland.

How is this a great yūgen poem? But even before asking that, one might ask: Why quail—or bobwhite? And what is the image or the atmosphere that the poem is supposed to create?

My wife Nancy, who often heard bobwhites outside our rental cottage during summer vacations in Montauk, at the eastern tip of Long Island, around 1980, characterizes their calls as "friendly, cheerful." But the Japanese variety of quail (*Coturnix japonica*), now on the red list, seems to make delicate, plaintive calls.

Meanwhile, books tell us that in English literature the quail, because of its "supposed amorous disposition," as the *O.E.D.* puts it, is a metaphor for a courtesan or prostitute, as when Shakespeare, in his *Troilus and Cressida*, makes the foul-mouthed Thersites grumble (V. i.), "Here's Agamemnon, an honest fellow enough, and one / that loves quails, but he has not so much brain as / ear-wax."

If the quail has had any amorous association in Japanese imagination, it is rather of a forlorn, sad sort. An inhabitant of grasslands, the migrant from Siberia began by evoking a barren, desolate area where few human beings lived. And its rather plaintive calls—the bird "crows," too—intensified its sense of solitude. So, even though it breeds during the summer, the quail began to become an autumnal image.

In the *Man'yōshū*, the phrase *uzura-naku*, "quail-calling" or "where quails call," settled down as an epithet for "old," "ancient," "past," or even "decrepit." Here is a love poem Ōtomo no Yakamochi (718 – 85) sent to Ki no Iratsume (dates uncertain):

鶉鳴く故りにし郷ゆ思へどもなにそも妹に逢ふよしもなき

Though thinking of you since the quail-calling olden home, why no means of meeting you?

The "olden home" refers to the Heijō-kyō, the palace quarters in Nara. Emperor Shōmu (701–56) moved out of Nara and set up his administrative post in Kuni-kyō, in today's Kyoto, in 740, keeping it there until 744. That was where Yakamochi happened to be when he wrote the poem. So you might say Yakamochi exaggerated a bit to use the epithet, "quail-calling."

That, then, is the origin of Shunzei's image. More directly, the atmosphere he tried to create in this poem may be understood a little better by taking into account Episode 123 of *Tales of Ise*. It reads in its entirety:

Once there was a man. He must have felt that he was finally tiring of the woman who lived in Deep Grass, for he made a poem that went like this:

年をへて住みこし里を出でていなばいとゞ深草野
とやなりなん

If I go out of this village I've lived in for years
it will become a very Deep Grass field

The woman, in reply:

野とならば鶉となりて鳴きおらんかりにだにやは君
は来ざらむ

If it becomes a field I'll become a quail and
keep calling just in case you come to hunt

Touched by this, he lost the heart to leave her.

By suggesting this vignette as the background of his poem, Shunzei, in effect, wrote a follow-up on an old amatory tale. In so doing, he created a poem of autumnal desolation.

Shunzei's poem, as a great poetic arbiter's own choice, went on to be accepted as *the* exemplar of "ineffable, yes, ineffable" by the generations that followed. This—along with one of his tenets, that "the heart" of poetry was difficult to express in words—helped shape one conception of yūgen—a process subtly affected by the religious overtones Shunzei brought to bear on poetry.

In his book of poetics-cum-anthology *Korai fūtei shō* (*Overview of Poetic Styles Since Ancient Times*), Shunzei posited that a pursuit of poetry would lead to enlightenment. He took Buddhist vows at age sixty-two, in 1176, adopting the name Shaku'a. As he completed his treatise, "around the tenth of Seventh Month," in 1197, he did not fail to present himself as an ideal Buddhist hermit. He lives, he noted, in "a grass hut where the evening breeze is cool" and his "mossy sleeves"—of his ascetic robe—"grow soaked with dew every morning."

Perhaps it was expected, then, that Shunzei started to use *sabi* as a virtue by which to judge a poem. The meanings of *sabi* largely come from *sabishi*, "lonely," "desolate," "neglected," but also from *sabiru*,

"Heart of the Shadow"
Photograph by Juna Amano

"to rust," so that, according to *Ruisenshū* (*Collection of Similar Boats*), a book of *haikai* associations compiled in 1676, it was linked to shrines, old men, swords and other things made of metal, manmade gardens, and even lacquerware. *Sabi* as a poetic and therefore aesthetic standard readily converged with *wabi*, which comes from *wabishi*, "inconsolably lonely," "painful," "desolate." And it was *wabi* that Murata Shukō (1422?–1502) and Sen no Rikyū (1522–91) would emphasize in the art of drinking tea and that Matsuo Bashō is strongly associated with in his *hokku*, today known as haiku.

One important way of promulgating an aesthetic notion in poetry in Shunzei's days was to use it as a criteria in *uta-awase*, tanka matches.

Uta-awase began, at the latest, in the ninth century. At first, like most other competitive things the leisurely courtiers did outside their government duties, it was a game. In time, though, subjecting pairs of poems to judgment in order to determine winners and losers became a formal affair. For each such contest a judge was selected, two teams of poets, each led by a captain, were lined up, and often the emperor or some other member of the imperial family presided. The poems were composed on topics given in advance, the place for the contest was prepared with care, and the participants presented themselves in formal attire. Usually the judge had the final say, but sometimes members of each team were allowed to argue for the compositions on their side or against those on the other side.

As diction, allusion, phrasing, and such were analyzed with ever greater sophistication, certain aesthetic notions began to hold sway. Yūgen was one of them, and Fujiwara no Shunzei became its greatest promoter in poetry. In the records left of the proceedings of the contests in which Shunzei was judge, fourteen cases are known where he cited the term in making his judgment. Of the poems cited, the one by Monk Saigyō (1118–90) prompted Shunzei to observe: "its heart is yūgen; the manner of its enunciation cannot be excelled."

こころなき身にも哀はしられけりしぎたつ沢の秋の夕暮
Even to the heartless being pity is known: snipes rise from a marsh this autumn evening

What does "the heartless being" (*kokoro-naki mi*) mean? Because Saigyō abandoned his samurai status to take Buddhist vows at the manful prime of twenty-two, it is usually assumed to refer to a mind able to transcend "sorrow and joy, love and hatred" (Japanese: *bonnō*, Sanskrit: *klesa*, sometimes translated "passions"), and most translators follow that assumption: Earl Miner, "While denying his heart, / Even a priest must feel his body know" *etc.*; William LaFleur, "Thought I was free / Of passions": Burton Watson: "Even a person free of passion"; and Gustav Heldt: "With a heart dead to the world."

But the phrase *kokoro-naki* on its own also means "unfeeling," "uncultivated," "lacking in poetic sensibility," and some interpreters of this poem apply that meaning here.

In any event, the poem went on to win great fame. For one thing, it seems to illuminate Saigyō the man supremely well—a devout Buddhist unable to transcend secular attachments, including poetic sensibility. For another, in the *Shin-Kokinwakashū* (*New Collection of Poems Ancient and Modern*), compiled in 1205, the poem was ensconced between two other poems on "autumn evening," both of which Shunzei would have approved as equally effective exemplars of yūgen:

さびしさはその色としもなかりけり真木たつ山の秋の夕
暮

Loneliness has no particular color: black pines
rise on the mountain this autumn evening

こころなき身にも哀はしられけりしぎたつ沢の秋の夕暮
Even to the heartless being pity is known: snipes
rise from the marsh this autumn evening

見わたせば花も紅葉もなかりけり浦のとまやの秋の夕
暮

As I look out there are neither blossoms nor
maple leaves: by a cove a thatched hut this
autumn evening

Of these three, known as the *sanseki*,
"The Three Evenings," the first is by Monk
Jakuren (1139?–1202), Shunzei's nephew
adopted as his son. The third is by Shunzei's
real son, Teika, whom we met earlier. Teika's
poem, which would become a favorite among
artists in various fields, brings to mind one
of Shun'e's attempts to define yūgen cited
earlier, to wit:

. . . the way the evening sky appears in
autumn, it has neither color nor voice. Still,

although you cannot tell wherefore and for what reason, tears well up and never cease. Those with no heart think nothing of this, loving as they do only [cherry] blossoms and maple leaves,

In fact, by Teika's time "neither blossoms nor maple leaves" had become a set phrase embodying aestheticism, with his poem harking back to the following passage in the "Akashi" chapter of *The Tale of Genji*:

. . . The sound of a musical instrument that is not especially remarkable can be marvelous, depending on the occasion. Here, there was the sea, stretching far into the distance with nothing interfering, and though there were no blossoms nor maple leaves of spring or autumn at their best, the shadows of plants simply growing here and there looked all the more sensuous. . . .

Akashi is where Genji the Shining Prince moves from Suma, another seashore village to the east to which he had exiled himself following political and amatory turmoil in the Capital, that is, Kyoto. This is a scene where the Lay Priest of Akashi, who wants to "offer" his daughter to Genji, comes to visit with some musical instruments, "on a tranquil moonlit night."

The proposition, "neither blossoms nor maple leaves," gives us occasion to think about the role of *yojō* (*yozei*), "overtones," or *omokage*, "suggestiveness," in understanding yūgen. Trying to define yūgen, Shun'e spoke of the ability "to set forth a profound feeling without revealing it, to conjure in your mind a world you haven't seen, to manifest elegance in the guise of the base, and to project the subtlest logic while looking foolish." It may not be surprising to learn, then, that he was led to conclude: "The color white, though without any special luster, is superior to all other colors."

The renga master Monk Shinkei (1406–75) went a step further, perhaps, when he said, while equating yūgen with "overtones" (*yozei*) in his treatise *Sasamegoto* (*Idle Talks*), that yūgen lies in "what is left unsaid and has no logic," and that "the ultimate" in poetry is "to sing only of suggestiveness (*omokage*), in the style of non-clarity." To illustrate what he meant, he referred to the following passage from *Tsurezuregusa* (*Essays in Idleness*), of the essayist-poet Yoshida Kenkō (1283–1352):

> How can we say we must look at the [cherry] blossoms only in full bloom, the moon only when it's spotless? It moves you more, makes you feel more deeply, to long for the moon when it's raining or not to know spring's whereabouts with all your blinds down. There is more to see in a tree about to bloom or in the garden where blossoms, scattered, are wilting . . .

It may be said that this line of thinking eventually led the *haikai* poet Uejima Onitsura (1661–1738) to make, in his *Hitori-goto* (*Monologue*), a pronouncement that is paradoxical in the manner of Zen: "It should be difficult for a *yūgen* poem by someone accomplished to be understood by someone *un*accomplished, even opaquely. Because the words are so easy that the *un*accomplished person is likely to think anyone can do it."

Onitsura, a serious student of Zen, is best known for his *hokku*, which comes with a headnote:

When Monk Kūdō asked, "What is your haikai eye?" I responded on the spot:

庭前に白く咲いたる椿かな
In the garden blooming white: camellias

The proposition, "neither blossoms nor maple leaves," also gives us a chance to reflect on one of Liza Dalby's definitions of yūgen: "The *'kū'* of *'shiki soku ze kū.'*" Ms. Dalby refers, of course, to the most famous assertion in the short Buddhist text called the Heart Sutra (*Prajna-paramita-hrdayam samaptam*). In a Chinese translation of what is originally written in Sanskrit, it says 色即是空, and Ms. Dalby cites it in a Japanese reading, romanized. In the greatest modern Zen proselytizer Daisetz Suzuki's English translation, in *Manual of Zen Buddhism* (1960), the phrase becomes "form is here emptiness."

This is immediately followed by 空即是色 "emptiness is form."

To translate the corresponding passage in the Sanskrit original from a Japanese translation (interpretation) by Nakamura Hajime and Kino Kazuyoshi, who note that the famous Chinese translation skimps on the original, it may be given:

In this world, material phenomena have no substance; because they have no substance, they can be material phenomena. Having no substance does not mean they are separated from material phenomena. Also, material phenomena are not material phenomena by being separated from having no substance. Thus, on the whole, any material phenomenon means having no substance. On the whole, having no substance means a material phenomenon.

Ms. Dalby says that for her, yūgen is the "emptiness" of "form is emptiness." Suzuki explains:

"Water Stone" by Isamu Noguchi
Photograph by Bruce Schwarz

"Empty" (*sanya*) or "emptiness" (*sunyata*) is one of the most important notions in Mahayana philosophy. . . . Emptiness does not mean "relativity," or "phenomenality," or "nothingness," but rather means the Absolute, or something of transcendental nature. . . .

For that matter, here's Suzuki's attempt to define yūgen, in *Zen and Japanese Culture* (1959):

Yūgen is a compound word, each part, *yū* and *gen*, meaning "cloudy impenetrability," and the combination meaning "obscurity," "unknow*abi*lity," "mystery," "beyond intellectual calculability," but not "utter darkness." An object so designated is not subject to dialectical analysis or to a clear-cut definition. It is not at all presentable to our sense-intellect as this or that, but this does not mean. . . .

But we are ahead of ourselves.

First, even as yūgen as an aesthetic value in poetry seemed to deepen its sense of "ineffable," "mysterious," "unfathomable," the term of similar praise which, apparently contradictory, at times seemed interchangeable with it coexisted: *en* (艶), "lustrous." Shunzei made one famous pronouncement in this regard when he talked about poetry in general. "Either simply reading out a poem or making one, it should sound somehow both *en* and yūgen," he wrote.

Another pronouncement of his that's quoted as often is his judgment in a pair during "The 1,500-Round Poetry Matches," held in 1202:

風吹けば花の白雲やゝ消えて夜な夜なはるゝ三吉野の
　月

As wind blows the white clouds of blossoms fade
　　somewhat, nightly clearing the Yoshino moon

Making this poem—by Retired Emperor Gotoba—the winner over the one matched with it, Shunzei observed that "the Yoshino moon clearing night by night might suggest more *en* than the utterly spotless autumn sky," because "in the Way of Poetry (*uta no michi*) I would suggest that something like the Yoshino moon clearing nightly did not attain yūgen." Talk of being circumlocutory!

Anyway, the term en was also expressed by words like *gien* (妓艶), *yōen* (妖艶), *yūen* (優艶), any of which in turn may mean "fragile," "touching," "gentle," "refined," "resplendent," or "expansive and vague." It was to be expected, then, that Nijō Kaneyo (1250–1338), who compiled the fifteenth Imperial anthology, should have advocated *karei yūgen* (花麗幽玄), "yūgen of flowery elegance," as the ideal in poetry.

And that brings us to the one other important person to look at to gain a classical understanding of yūgen: Zeami Motokiyo.

Dr. *H*— took me to a *nō* performance. These are extremely interesting old plays. . . . The arrangement of stage, actors, chairs, musicians, etc., remind one partly of the old Greek plays and partly of the original Shakespearean style of acting. There is no scenery, but one pine tree and a few necessary implements. . . .

The performance began at 9 in the morning, but I was there soon after half-past eight to see the audience come in. There was no artificial light, and as it poured with rain it was at times rather dark, and the rain came in in places. . . .

—Marie Stopes,
Entry on November 3, 1907,
A Journal from Japan

Mr. Ezra Pound has found among the Fenollosa manuscripts a story traditional among Japanese [nō] players. A young man was following a stately old woman through the streets of a Japanese town, and presently she turned to him and spoke: "Why do you follow me?" "Because you are so interesting." "That is not so, I am too old to be interesting." But he wished, he told her, to become a player of old women on the Noh stage. If he would become famous as a Noh player, she said, he must not observe life, nor put on an old voice and stint the music of his voice. He must know how to suggest an old woman and yet find it all in the heart.

—William Butler Yeats,
Introduction to Certain Noble Plays of Japan, 1916

Noh is an exceedingly slow and deliberate style of drama. Each step of the foot and each gesture of the hand are carefully measured and stylized. Maximum economy of gesture and movement and complete restraint characterize a performance. A step can mean a complete journey; the lifting of the hand, weeping; the merest turn of the head, negation. *Noh* abounds in understatement.... The curious enjoyment of a *Noh* performance lies in the fact that afterwards, in retrospect, after the strain and chore of following minutely its poetry and its elusive gestures are over, the lyric overtones penetrate and move the spectator's heart.

—Faubion Bowers
Japanese Theatre, 1952

With the nō drama actor-writer-theorist Zeami Motokiyo, we enter, in a more obviously paradoxical manner, a dichotomous realm of yūgen, at once luminous and tenebrous.

Let us briefly review nō and Zeami's relationship to it.

Nō grew out of a jumble of festival or religious performing arts imported from China and initially included mime, song, dance, acrobatics, and magic. It was called Sangaku, a Japanese pronunciation of *sanyue*, the Chinese name for such performances, which are said to have traveled all the way from the Middle East to China. At first, the Japanese government designated performers for them, but not long afterward abolished the profession, apparently because their popularity rendered government support unnecessary. Later, the performers included a class of outcasts. In time, perhaps because miming was stressed and the monkey is regarded as a great mimic, the name changed to Sarugaku, "monkey entertainment." Also, a variation called Dengaku, "paddy entertainment," was born. The name nō came into being by the thirteenth century, but the name Sarugaku and Dengaku survived for some time afterward.

Nō was recognized as worthy of elite attention when the third Ashikaga shogun Yoshimitsu (1358–1408) discovered the talent of Zeami's father, Kan'ami Kiyotsugu (1333–84), and patronized him and his son. By all contemporary accounts, Yoshimitsu *loved* Zeami as a boy—beautiful to behold and talented. The shogun's love prompted many of his ranking vassals to lavish attention on Zeami; so did, among aristocrats, the poet Nijō Yoshimoto (1320–88). Yoshimoto, who laid down the first set of coherent rules for renga, devised for Zeami one of his early names, Fujiwaka, "Wisteria Youth."

For Zeami, shogunate patronage was crucial—far more so than aristocratic patronage was for, let us say, Shakespeare. When Yoshimitsu died and the succeeding shogun, Yoshimochi, turned his attention to another actor, Zeami had to struggle for the survival of his troupe. The fifth shogun Yoshinori even maltreated him and his troupe, in the end exiling him for reasons that remain unclear. Zeami was by then past seventy years of age. Little is known about the remainder of his life. It is difficult to imagine anything similar happening to Shakespeare as a result of the loss of favor of, say, William Herbert, the Earl of Pembroke — though here the analogy may be skewed because Herbert is neither Queen Elizabeth or King James.

For Zeami, who perfected the art of nō as we know it today, the need to hold shogunate or nobles' attention meant an up-front stress on elegance. Throughout his writings on nō he almost obsessively used two words: *hana* 花, "flower," and *yūgen*.

What did Zeami mean by "flower"? What did he mean when he said, "The flower is the life of nō"?

In his day, the flower was the supreme

symbol of upper-class elegance. When Zeami the stage actor used it in his argument, however, he had something practical and immediate in mind. For him, it meant the ability to catch the eye and charm the spectator, as a flower does. And the one important ramification of this attribute of the flower as Zeami saw it was readiness, as when Hamlet said, "the readiness is all."

In *Fūshi kaden* (*Style and Flower*), Zeami observes:

> . . . in the Sarugaku [performed] for a religious purpose or in front of a noble, with a large crowd assembling, the seating area may not be quiet. At such a time, the actor should remain quiet, very quiet, until the spectators, impatient for his performance, focus their thousand minds on one thing and direct their gaze to the greenroom, wondering, "Why is he being so slow?" The actor should seize that moment, step out, and enunciate his first line. At once, the spectators will fall in line, and the minds of the thousands will harmonize with the actor's move and empathize with him. . . .

Nonetheless, because Sarugaku basically assumes the attendance of a noble, should he come early, it wouldn't do *not* to start at once. At such a time, the spectators may not yet have settled down in their seats. Some, being late, may still be standing about, lost, the minds of the thousands not yet focused on nō. . . . At such a time, the actor should be more emphatic in his gestures, stronger in his voice, raise his legs higher in stomping, and on the whole try to be more vivid in action than usual, so he may attract attention. . . .

Zeami goes on to describe various other situations, among them one in which troupes compete. In those days, theatrical events were often daylong affairs which at times went on into the night, with several troupes taking the stage by turns, the spectators coming and going. For Zeami, the flower was the ability to deal successfully with each situation—although it must be added that his conception of the flower included that of a wilting one. As he puts it, to paraphrase somewhat, "The wilting flower should be placed above the flower abloom."

He defines yūgen or what it means to him in unmistakable terms. In *Kakyō* (*Flower Mirror*), he says:

. . . as to what's called the realm of yūgen, where should it be situated? First, to take an example from the world as we know it and look at all the various kinds of people, one must say that the noble attains the rank of yūgen in the way he holds himself loftily and wins trust and admiration in a manner different from the rest of the world.

This being the case, being simply beautiful and gracious is the essence of yūgen. Holding your body peacefully is the yūgen of the performing body. Again, being graceful in speech, by closely observing and thoroughly mastering the customary way of speaking of the noble and highborn, so that even the casual words that come out of your mouth may be graceful, that has to be the yūgen of speech. . . .

Putting yourself in the role you play, no matter what role you may change yourself into, you must not separate yourself from yūgen. Be it someone of the high class or someone of the low class, a man or a woman, a monk or a layman, a farmer or a peasant, a beggar or an outcast, you must appear as if you were holding a spray of flowers in your hand....

This "flower" is the performing body.

Little wonder the American scholar J. Thomas Rimer and the Japanese playwright Yamazaki Masakazu chose the word "grace" for yūgen when they translated Zeami's treatises in *On the Art of nō Drama* (1984). (I use their English translations of titles in referring to Zeami's treatises.)

Indeed, one of the images Zeami chose for yūgen expresses his idea of "grace" in striking fashion: "snow in a silver bowl." He selected this image when he divided stages of development in acting ability into nine levels (*Kyūi*, the title of his treatise on the subject) and sought to define pictorially the lowest of the top three, which was where he argued yūgen was achieved. The phrase of course has Chinese sources, among them *Biyanlu* (*The Blue Cliff Record*), a collection of Zen observations compiled in 1125. In R. D. M. Shaw's translation (1961), which retains

Japanese pronunciations of Chinese names and phrases, the relevant passage reads:

> "The inside of the silver bowl is heaped with snow." This is a quotation from Tō-san's *Treasure Mirror Meditation* (*Ho Kyo Sammika*). The full quotation is: The silver bowl is heaped with snow; the bright moonlight shimmers round the white heron. Varied yet similar, blended yet distinguishable.

In response to Zeami's "snow in a silver bowl," John Gillespie, a college professor turned business consultant and the author, with Robert Rolf, of *Alternative Japanese Drama* (1992), cites the nō play *Himuro* (*Ice Storage Room*) as illustrative of Zeami's "elusive notion of yūgen (that which lies under the surface)." He explains:

> . . . It is a story of ice somehow preserved even during the heat of summer. "Ordinary ice," intones the *waki*, "before the rising winds of spring, / will thaw and melt away." The chorus reflects his wonderment at the staying power of this special snow and ice:

"how can the snow, I wonder, / still remain unthawed?" This snow/ice that should, but does not, thaw in summer is personified in the *shite*, a divinity embodying the spirit of the purity in ice. The oddness of ice not melting, even in summer, is enhanced by the *shite* wearing the demon mask *beshimi akujo*. The contrast between his purity as ice god and his demonic aspect surely reflects the polarities in nature between cold and heat, which, though extreme, are complementary in nature's grand cycle. . . .

We will see in a while what the *waki* and *shite* are.

One other image I must not fail to overlook in Zeami's thinking is the one given in a poem by Fujiwara no Teika. It occurs in a passage in *Yūgaku shūdō fūken* (*Disciplines for Joy*), where Zeami discusses the Heart Sutra observation quoted earlier: "Form is here emptiness; emptiness is form."

駒とめて袖うちはらふかげもなしさののわたりの雪
の夕暮

No shelter for halting the horse to brush off
my sleeves, here at Sano Ferry this snowy
evening

This is Teika's masterpiece. Being a masterpiece, it fascinates me, but I cannot tell *how*
it does this. As I understand it, it appears to
describe simply what happened on a road
when the poet, while traveling, with the snow
falling, couldn't even find shelter to stop in.
But, ignorant as I am of the way of poetry,
I thought there might be some other way
this poem moves us and asked an expert, but
was told it is just as it is. I don't think that
the poet had the thought of appreciating the
snow; rather, finding himself in a place with
no visibility, where he was unable to tell his
whereabouts from a mountain or a river, and
lost on a road with no shelter to stop in, he
just happened to say this, or so it seems to
me.

What someone truly accomplished does
must have a similar feeling, which can't be
expressed. . . . In our art, too, when someone
attains mastery, he, like "No shelter for halting

the horse," will evince no artfulness, pay no
attention to appearances, but will simply
reveal a feeling that is no feeling, an appearance
that is detached from appearance. . . .

So, that is the ultimate state.

Still, if Zeami's view of nō is that it has to
be as luminous as a flower abloom—and that
it has to be seen; as he makes clear at one
point in *Fūshi kaden*, not for him is a flower
"born to blush unseen, / And waste its sweet-
ness on the desert air"—that it has to be the
snow in a silver bowl, where does the association of nō with something tenebrous, som-
ber, mysterious, or ambiguous come from?

Sitting as sole judge in "The 600-Round Poetry Matches," held in 1193, Fujiwara no Shunzei famously observed:

> . . . Lady Murasaki excels as a poetry-writer but even more so as a prose writer. Moreover, "Hana no en" ("Flower Banquet") in particular stands out for its elegance. A poet who doesn't look at [*The Tale of*] *Genji* is truly deplorable.

Shunzei said this in making the following poem, one of a pair, the winner:

見し秋を何に残さん草の原ひとつにかはる野べのけし
  きに

> In what shall I leave the autumn I've seen when the field of grass becomes a single hue?

Here, the suggestion is that "the field of grass" is a field carpeted with multitudes of colorful wildflowers. This poem, Shunzei decided, alludes, subtly, indirectly, to the poem a young woman, agitated, makes when a tipsy Genji corners her and asks her name:

うき身世にやがて消えなば尋ねても草の原をば問はじ
　とや思ふ

If I fade soon, unhappily, would you ask, wouldn't
　you inquire after me in a field of grass?

In this poem, "a field of grass" is a
metaphor for the place of burial. It is when
Genji's deep involvement with this young
woman, named Oborozukiyo ("Blurred
Moonlight"), is revealed that Genji is forced
to exile himself to Suma, then to Akashi.

Shunzei's reverence for *The Tale of Genji* as
a source of poetic inspiration and aesthetics
was such that it once prompted Minamoto
no Chikayuki (dates uncertain), a much
younger poet, to confine himself in a room
and read a particular chapter of the tale sixty
times, according to his own testimony. There
were other narratives that were important
for poets, among them *Tales of Ise*, but *Genji*
had a special place—at least for those who
came under the influence of Shunzei and his
thought.

Zeami the dramatist was one of them.
Like other nō writers, he based most of his

dramas on legends as well as existing tales and poems. (For example, *Sekidera Komachi* pivots on a single poem of Ono no Komachi.) And, from the perspective of our inquiry into something tenebrous and mysterious that we associate with nō, Zeami's most telling reference to *Genji* in relation to his idea of yūgen appears in his treatise *Sandō: Nōsakusho* (*The Three Elements in Composing a Play*). In a passage where he discusses "the ultimate rank of yūgen" that may be attained by depicting noblewomen, he lists, as "the jewels among the jewels," three characters from *Genji*: "Lady Rokujō possessing and tormenting Lady Aoi, Yūgao taken by a spirit, and Ukifune possessed."

Now, as Doris Bargen reminds us in her book, *A Woman's Weapon*, Lady Murasaki's novel is usually remembered for "its delicately drawn characterizations" of those who peopled the tenth-century Japanese court, but not for its "highly dramatic, violently animated, narratively important episodes of female discontent." In this view of *The Tale of Genji*, Zeami apparently was someone who held an unusual opinion, though he may well have gotten it all wrong. The three characters he listed as most appropriate for nō drama are among the five paragons of female discontent Bargen chose for her erudite analysis.

Who are they? What do they do? What happens to them?

Rokujō—more fully, Rokujō no Miya-sundokoro or the Imperial Bedchamber of Sixth Avenue, "the Imperial bedchamber" designating a lady who serves the Emperor in his bed or, as here, the wife of a Crown Prince)—is a widow, with a daughter, of a Crown Prince. Genji, still in his teens but already married for some years, sets out to seduce her. She at first resists, but in the end succumbs. Thereupon, Genji loses interest. As he muses at one point, she is "so deeply loving" that it sometimes becomes "stifling" to be with her.

One year, during the Aoi (Birthwort) Festival, Rokujō goes out to see it, with some reluctance. The Shining Prince is to play a splendid role in it. Yes, she resents him for neglecting her, but she still loves him and she hopes to have a glimpse of him. As it turns out, the servants tending the carriage of Genji's wife, Aoi no Ue—*no ue* indicates higher rank; Aoi is the first daughter of the Minister of the Left and a younger sister of Emperor Suzaku, Genji's older brother by a different mother—humiliate Rokujō by manhandling her carriage at the viewing stand. If the news earlier of Aoi's pregnancy had made her jealous, this public humiliation is too much to take.

When Aoi falls ill and the rumor reaches Rokujō that her spirit is torturing Genji's wife, she becomes anguished. "I do worry about myself and lament my fate," she tells herself, "but I have no wish to do other people harm. Still, a soul, while brooding, might indeed wander off (to someone else)." She also has nightmares in which she "pulls Aoi around" and "strikes her." Aoi dies after giving birth to a boy in her illness. The suggestion is that Rokujō killed her. Such troubles persuade her to leave Kyoto for Ise—by taking advantage of the appointment of her daughter as vestal of the Ise Shrine. On her way there, Genji visits her at Nonomiya, the Field Shrine, where purification rites are conducted for her daughter.

Long after Aoi's death, Rokujō's spirit also appears at the death of Murasaki, another of Genji's wives and the most beloved—and, again, when Onna Sannomiya ("Third Princess"), still another wife, takes Buddhist vows.

Yūgao ("Moonflower") is a woman Genji discovers while still visiting Rokujō. He moves her from her wretched abode to an abandoned mansion of a nobleman. There, on the night of the second day of love-making, she suddenly dies of fright just after Genji sees, while dozing, a beautiful woman sitting near his pillow and hears her remonstrate: "I admire you for being so wonderful, but you don't come to visit me. Instead, you bring in an ordinary woman like this and indulge her. I hadn't expected anything like this and it pains my heart." (Or, as Arthur Waley put it: "You who think yourself so fine, how comes it that you have brought to toy with you here this worthless common creature, picked up at random in the streets? I am astonished and displeased.") The apparition in Genji's dream is thought to be Rokujō's.

Afterward, Genji learns that Yūgao had banished herself after learning about the displeasure of her lover's wife, and also that she had left a daughter. The daughter's name is Tamakazura ("Beautiful Vine"). When Genji finds her, he adopts her, but then makes amorous advances, which troubles her greatly.

Ukifune ("Floating Boat") is a character who appears after Genji's death.

A beautiful daughter of an imperial prince who lives in Uji, outside Kyoto, Ukifune is pursued by two attractive men: Genji's son, Kaoru ("Fragrance")—in truth, the son of his wife Onna Sannomiya and another man—and an imperial prince, Niou ("Scent"). Loving both men, Ukifune grows anxious about her entanglements until, finally, she decides to kill herself by throwing herself into the torrential Uji River. After she leaves her house, however, a spirit apparently possesses her and she loses consciousness. She is found sprawled under a large tree, weeping, unaware of where she is or who she is.

Ukifune regains consciousness more or less when the spirit said to be possessing her is removed through prayers and a medium (who screams, "Because this woman resented the world from the bottom of her heart and kept saying day and night, 'How can I die?' I took advantage of that and took possession of her one very dark night when she was alone!"). She then decides to pursue a religious way of life and eventually becomes a nun.

What such anxieties and nightmares may mean from modern anthropological and psychological perspectives is the focus of Doris Bargen's study, *A Woman's Weapon*. Well, then, how do nō plays treat these women—victims, if you will, of a polygynous society? There are at least four dramas dealing with them in the classical repertoire: *Aoi no Ue, Nonomiya, Yūgao,* and *Ukifune*.

All nō plays are short. A recent edition of "100 nō plays" (*Yōkyoku hyakuban*, 1998) is a single volume of 640 pages, even with an introduction to each play and adequate footnotes. The original edition, published in 1631, required twenty volumes, but that was because printing was done in generous fashion in those days.

Almost all nō plays are simply constructed—usually with two acts, often with a narrative intermission. Excluding the chorus, there are basically only two players: *shite*, the main actor, and *waki*, the secondary or companion actor. In almost all cases, the waki first appears to introduce the setting. The shite then appears. The waki sees her and asks some questions. The shite tells a suggestive story and disappears. That's the first act. In the second act, the shite appears again, but this time as the protagonist of the story she told. The shite usually wears a mask and sometimes changes masks in the second act. In almost all cases, all roles are traditionally played by men.

Around 1930 a scholar of nō came up with a rubric for a certain type of play: *mugen nō*, "nō of dream and illusion." It refers to the loose group of narratives in which the painful part of the protagonist's life is relived, reenacted by her apparition, in a dream or hallucination or in a shamanistic or sorcerous setting—for catharsis, salvation, expiation, or for the simple venting of emotions arising from a perceived misunderstanding or emotions left unconveyed. Zeami is said to have perfected this latterly invented category of nō, and in it generally fall the four plays dealing with Rokujō, Yūgao, and Ukifune that I have cited.

"Dream" and "illusion" are both Buddhist metaphors for the transience of all things, of all beings. A passage from the Vimalakirti Nirdesa Sutra says: "Manjusri asked Vimalakirti: 'How should a Bodhisattva look at living beings?' Vimalakirti replied: 'A Bodhisattva should look at living beings like an illusionist does at the illusory men (he has created) . . . at a sleeping man seeing he is awake in a dream. . . .'"

Borrowing this notion, Lady Izumi (born 970s), Murasaki's colleague at the court, composed a poem on love. It comes with a headnote.

I sent this poem to a man whom I met and loved for the duration of dew:

白露も夢もこの世もまぼろしもたとへていえばひさ
しかりけり
White dew, dreams, this world, illusions: all these
last for eternities in comparison

—in comparison, that is, with love.

The three women from *Genji* whom Zeami called "the jewels among the jewels" embodying yūgen, as interpreted for the nō stage—"Lady Rokujō possessing and tormenting Lady Aoi, Yūgao taken by a spirit, and Ukifune possessed"—are deeply, hopelessly, troubled souls. The yūgen of nō is at once luminous and tenebrous, because there is a schism, by design, between the external ideal of grace and elegance and the internal reality of suffering and torment.

So, let us look at how nō dramatists interpreted the three women in four plays, with this in mind: these represent only a small part of mugen nō. In reading each of these synopses, imagine a stage with "no scenery, but one pine tree and a few necessary implements" and the main actor in a gorgeous, resplendent costume.

Aoi no Ue
Book, as revised by Zeami

(A stagehand brings out a folded kimono and places it on the floor close to the apron. It represents the ailing Aoi.)

A subject of Retired Emperor Suzaku appears and reports that Aoi, the daughter of the Minister of the Left, is possessed by a spirit, and that "noble priests and high priests were summoned" to pray for her, to no avail. Now a reputable female shaman has been summoned to tell whether Aoi is possessed by "the spirit of someone alive or the spirit of someone dead."

The shaman appears and repeats her magic words.

Rokujō comes on stage like a shadow, in a movement that suggests she is riding in a broken carriage. *(No prop is used.)* As she wonders aloud if she could "get out of the burning house." (The burning house is a metaphor for this world—in which people enjoy themselves heedless of the calamity about to engulf them. "Simile and Parable," of the Lotus Sutra.) She mentions the name Yūgao. She announces that yes, she is indeed Rokujō's wraith. Once, while she was the Crown Prince's consort, she enjoyed every fabulous moment of the court; now, she's "a wilted morning-glory simply waiting for the sun to set." Yes, she has "appeared to vent resentments," she says, and proceeds to the kimono laid on the floor and strikes it with her fan.

In the semi-intermission, it is decided to summon a holy man. While this is being done, Rokujō, on stage, changes to a hannya *mask which shows a face contorted with demonic thoughts.*

The holy man appears, seats himself next to the kimono representing Aoi, and begins to pray for her soul. A fierce struggle ensues between the praying holy priest and the vengeful Rokujō. At one point, when Rokujō manages to approach Aoi's bed again, she's struck by the priest with his rosary. In the end, the priest's prayers work to "calm Rokujō's demonic soul," and Bodhisattvas descend from heaven to welcome her to Nirvana.

Nonomiya
Book by Komparu Zenchiku

(A torii is set up on the main stage.)
A traveling priest appears and says: He's seen "all the famous places and ancient relics in Kyoto and the autumn is late," so he will take a look at the relic of Nonomiya, the Field Shrine. At the site, a young woman appears and speaks, as if to herself, of "the autumnal desolation . . . now the thousands of wildflowers have all faded."

Kanze Hisao dancing *Nonomiya*
Photograph by Yoshikoshi Ken

Startled by "the sudden advent of a sensuous woman," the priest asks who she is. She evades the question, but tells him that he can't stay there because, though the purification rites for the Ise vestal hadn't been held for a long time, on the seventh of Ninth Month, which is today, every time she remembers what happened in the past, she comes here to clean the place.

The priest refuses to go, saying he's someone who "abandoned the world." So the woman tells how Genji the Shining Prince visited Rokujō there on this day and what he did. She explains who Rokujō was and how Genji had begun "visiting her unreasonably, in secret," after her husband, whom she loved, unexpectedly passed away. But "how someone's mind works is never known"; Genji then seldom visited her. . . .

Noticing that the woman telling this story is "no ordinary person," the priest—actually, the chorus—asks her name. She says she is "someone dead," that she is Rokujō herself. The woman then "disappears in the evening dusk, in the autumn wind, in the moonlight filtering through the trees of the forest, under the trees where the light is faint, behind the two pillars of the black-wood torii."

In the intermission a village man appears and, in response to the priest's request, tells him about Genji's visit with Rokujō at Nonomiya, and urges him to pray for her soul.

In the second act, Rokujō's ghost appears on a "flower carriage" adorned with the "thousand wildflowers of autumn." *(Except for some special staging, no prop suggesting a carriage is used.)* She then recalls how Aoi's servants humiliated her at the Aoi Festival and pleads with the priest to clear her mind of the resentment she still holds over the incident. As the priest prays, Rokujō's ghost dances, recalling the past, saying, "Both I, the visited, and he, the visitor, are mere dreams."

As she finishes her dance, whether she has managed to leave "the gate of the burning house" is left unanswered.

Yūgao
Book by someone in Zeami's circle

A priest appears and announces that he has arrived in Kyoto on his way to a famous shrine. Reaching Fifth Avenue, where Ariwara no Narihira once lamented, "Not the moon," etc., he comes upon a wretched house where he is puzzled to hear a woman reciting a poem. It is the poem Yūgao made when Genji took her to an unnamed mansion.

A young city woman emerges and vaguely hints at a love affair that did not last, suggesting that she is still pained by it. In the ensuing exchange with the priest, she points out that even though Lady Murasaki left the mansion in question unnamed, it was once the residence of a famous Minister of the Left. The priest says he is happy to see such a well-known place and besides to be able to offer prayers for the souls of Yūgao and her daughter, Tamakazura.

[Here, in an intratextual commentary on the source of this play, the woman adds: "In the first place, the tale of Genji the Shining

Prince is based on yūgen in diction and, though it may appear shallow in thought, it is in fact profound in meaning as it promotes bodhi (enlightenment) at its heart. . . . Above all, the volume of Yūgao stands out in excellence."]

The woman goes on to tell the story of Genji's relationships to Rokujō and Yūgao—that the latter was no more than a woman Genji happened to find on his way to see Rokujō. Yūgao, in truth, was like "a lamp flickering in a wind," who "dissipated like a bubble on the water." As she says this, she herself "disappears as if erased."

In the intermission, a man appears to tell the story of Genji and Yūgao in response to the priest's query. The priest tells him what he has just seen, and the man says the woman must have been Yūgao's apparition and urges the priest to pray for her soul.

In the second act, as the priest recites prayers, Yūgao's ghost appears and asks, "Please pray for me, now a ghost who dares reveal how a terrifying spirit vanquished a woman." As she dances, she thanks the priest for his prayers, and with "her smiling eyebrows opening up like the flower of the Dharma . . . she fades away among fragments of clouds, toward the dawning sky."

Ukifune
Book by "the amateur" Yokogoshi Motohisa
Music by Zeami

A traveling priest making a round of the provinces arrives in Uji, south of Kyoto, where he comes across a young woman on a boat carrying kindling. *(The only prop in this play is a stick the woman holds, which represents a pole.)* Asked what sort of person might have lived in Uji in the past, she replies, "I hear there once lived someone named Ukifune." The priest says, "Indeed, indeed, that's a story of Genji the Shining Prince." Asked to tell more about her, the woman says Ukifune was first loved by Kaoru, but was then inadvertently made love to by Prince Niou, whom Ukifune ended up "loving deeply," too. Lost and troubled, Ukifune wished to die and in the end did, "leaving not a trace, leaving not a trace."

Asked who she is, the woman gives a vague answer, though she hints she is still troubled by a spirit possessing her. She says she "must count on his power of the Dharma [to save her] and will wait for him over there," and disappears.

In the intermission, a village man appears, tells the priest the story of Ukifune in some detail, suggests that the woman he met must be her ghost, urges him to offer prayers for her soul, and exits.

In the second act, the priest announces he has decided to stay there overnight and offer prayers for Ukifune's soul. Ukifune's wraith appears. She says she is "a boat afloat with no set place to stay." As the priest prays, she tells, while dancing, how she was lost but saved by a priest by the grace of Kannon. The priest continues his prayers until, finally, she says she is now "cleared of her attachments" and "happy to be reborn in Tushita Heaven." Then she takes her leave, leaving only "a wind in the cedars" as the sky begins to lighten as the day breaks.

> *"Was it a vision,*
>   *or a waking dream?"*

So sang John Keats in "To a Nightingale."
Jorge Luis Borges wrote in *"Ars Poetica."*

> *Sentir que la vigilia es otro sueño*
> *Que sueña no soñar y que la muerte*
> *Que teme nuestra carne es esa muerte*
> *De cada noche, que se llama sueño.*
>
> *Ver en el día o en el año un símbolo*
> *De los días del hombre y de sus años,*
> *Convertir el ultaje de los años*
> *En una música un rumor y un símbolo....*

To feel that wakefulness is another dream
Dreaming it is not dreaming and that the death
Our flesh fears is that death
Which comes each night as sleep.

To see in the day or in the year a symbol
Of the days of man and of his years,
To transmute the atrocity of the years
Into a music a murmur and a symbol....
                              —*tr. Forrest Gander*

And among his set of haiku, he had this one:

¿Es o no es
El sueño que olvide
Antes de alba?

Is it or not
the dream I forgot
before dawn?

—*Tr. Andrea Cukier*

Lindley Williams Hubbell arrived in Japan, in 1953, and immersed himself in the work of Zeami Motokiyo, whose "genius" as "another great poet-playwright" had drawn him to the country. In the next forty years he saw, he told an interviewer just before his death, 186 out of the 240 plays in the classical repertoire of nō, some many times over. Such devotion to the stage art of nō may have come naturally to him: he had read all of Shakespeare by age ten, seen all of the major dramas in the Shakespeare Canon in his teens, and even played some of the bit parts with the troupe led by Robert Mantell (1854–1926).

There are Four Nō Troupes: the Kanze, Hōshō, Konparu, and Kongō. Mr. Hubbell supported the Kongō in particular that is noted for stressing splendor and elegance, as he deeply respected the troupe's 25th head, Kongō Iwao II (1924–1998).

Yet he remained reticent about this chosen form of theater in Japan, leaving only one or two program notes and (as far as I know) just two poems. The following is one of the poems. It was written for Teshima Yazaemon (1899–1978), the shite actor for the Kongō. Teshima's acting was at once resplendent, deep, and restrained, it was said. He was designated a Living National Treasure, in 1977.

Remembering Teshima-sensei

How simple a truly great artist can be!

For fifteen years Sensei and I were neighbors,
And when we met on the densha† he would bow,
Saluting me like an old gentleman from the country.
At such times I used to think:
What depths beyond depths of wisdom and
    creative power
Are lying there, perfectly relaxed,
In that man who, to an idle eye,
Might be an old farmer.
I cherish these memories
Now that his wisdom and his greatness
Have become a part of the universe.

---

† Streetcar, tramcar.

"Once"
Watercolor by Masaaki Noda

Monk Shinkei, the renga master, said in his *Teikin* (*Garden Teachings*): "What you maintain in mind is crucial. Be it when you see blossoms scattering or leaves falling or when you see dew on grass or tree, you must realize that this world is a dream, an illusion, you must behave graciously, you must keep yūgen in mind."

Bashō does not seem to have left any word on yūgen in writing or, for that matter, many words on *sabi*, either, although the latter concept is usually associated with his poetry. Nonetheless, some of his students and *haikai* practitioners who came later talked about either or both as something inseparable from Bashō's poetry. One such student was Morikawa Kyoriku (1656–1715). A samurai painter and *kanshi*-poet who is said to have been enlightened on *haikai* under Bashō, Kyoriku stated that "the *hosomi* of yūgen" was what he understood as the ultimate to be attained in *haikai*. He said this in *Honchō Monsen* (*A Japanese Anthology*), a collection of haibun, published in 1705. The following year, in his treatise-cum-list of *haikai* terms *Haikai Gagaku Shō* (1706), he elaborated:

> All phenomena move as substance in the void, but ought not to move as void in the substance. Substance is where you put yourself forward and resent others. For example, you sorrow over scattering blossoms and regret the declining moon. Regretting substance is the void of renga; regretting void is the substance of *haikai*. Above all, it is to lie skillfully in kanshi, waka [tanka], renga, and *haikai*. It's to show yourself in the void and impregnate your sentiments in the substance. . . .
>
> You ought to understand that the *haikai* of other schools is multicolored; the style of the Bashō school is like an ink-painting. . . .
>
> When it comes to the importance in devising a *hokku* in this school, first, the main thing is to follow the style of the Right School. This is to make pieces from what you see or hear. In this, not many aren't interesting. Therefore, you must add the *sabi • hosomi* of yūgen, thereby making people feel. For instance, if you talk about a farmer's

sentiments, it's standard to put wheat in a
· mortar; if you say you put yams (in a mortar)
is *sabi•hosomi*, etc.

The first part of the quotation translated
above may echo the Buddhist "material/no-
substance equal to substance/no-material"
transcendence.

Sabi, along with *hosomi*, "slenderness,"
"thinness," *shiori* and *shiorashiki*, the latter
two deriving from *shioru*, "to wilt," are the
haikai qualities that Tachibana Hokushi
(d. 1718) named as indispensable in *fūga*,
"poetry," in *Yamanaka Mondō* (*Questions and
Answers on the Mountains*). A sword-polisher,
Hokushi joined Bashō in the last leg of his
famed travels through the interior and wrote
the short book mainly quoting Bashō's state-
ments. It did not see print until 1850.

Kyoriku was Bashō's confidant and went
on to expound his spirit and aims in treatises
and anthologies after his death, so it is not-
able that he does not here discuss *karumi*,
"lightness," the aesthetic quality Bashō sought
in the last stage of his life as a *haikai* master.

I should add that *gagaku* in the title of Kyoriku's book refers to a dance-drama that came to Japan from the Asian Continent in the seventh century and was adopted for court and temple ceremonies. Here it's used in the sense of a means of peaceful governing, just as waka was, Bashō said, Kyoriku tells us.

I digress.

Kagami Shikō (1665–1731), equally eager in proselytizing "the Bashō style," though in less esoteric terms, saw an embodiment of yūgen in the most famous haiku of all time:

古池や蛙飛こむ水の音
An old pond: a frog leaps into the water the sound

A hundred years later, Takeuchi Gengen'-ichi (1742–1804), who compiled a collection of anecdotes about eccentrics among *hokku* writers in *Haika Kijin Dan* (*Episodes of Eccentrics among Haikai Poets*), had a somewhat different opinion on the matter. He rated the pond-frog *hokku* as attaining "the exquisite realm of Wang Wei," the Chinese poet (699–759) particularly famous for the quatrain, "Luchai" (Deer Corral):

In the vacant mountain I see no one,
only hear the sound of people talk.
The reflected sun comes in the deep wood,
again shining on the blue moss.

Gengen'ichi then cited the following as expressing "supreme yūgen":

花の雲鐘は上野か浅草か
Clouds of blossoms: Is the bell in Ueno or in
    Asakusa?

Cherry blossoms are traditionally appreciated in dreamlike profusions. That explains why, in 1912, as a token of friendship and gratitude to Theodore Roosevelt for making Japan the winner in the Russo-Japanese War, the City of Tokyo presented Washington DC with as many as three thousand cherry trees and New York with two thousand five hundred of them. In return, Washington

DC presented Tokyo with forty dogwoods, a more reasonable size as an arboreal gesture.

In 1687, Bashō, then living in Fukagawa, in Edo, wonders if the temple bell he hears is ringing in Ueno, which is to the northwest, or Asakusa, which is more or less to the north. Both were well known for cherry blossoms, and both had famous temples: Ueno, the shogunate temple Kan'ei-ji, and Asakusa, the popular Sensō-ji—*Sensō* being the sinified reading of *Asakusa*.

So, with Gengen'ichi we are back to the "flowery" view of yūgen.

About two hundred years later, Mishima Yukio (1925-1970) opened *Tennin gosui* (*The Five-Stage Decay of the Heavenly Being*), the last volume of his final work, the tetralogy *Hōjō no umi* (*The Sea of Fertility*), this way:

> The haze in the offing makes the distant ships appear yūgen. Still, the offing is clearer than yesterday, and you can trace the rims of the mountains of the Izu Peninsula. The sea of May is smooth. The sun is strong, the clouds faint, the sky blue.

Mishima, who was deeply immersed in classical Japanese literature and argued that all the aesthetic notions such as yūgen, *wabi*, and *sabi* flowed out of the ideal of *miyabi*, "courtly elegance," wrote this as he methodically orchestrated his own death.

The Tale of Genji, *Again*

Asked what comes to mind when she thinks of yūgen, Kakizaki Shōko, who studied Renaissance art and explicated Beethoven's Seventh Symphony at New York University, says, "Bagel."

Asked the same question, the poet Abe Hinako names Act II of *Giselle*, a ballet based on "a theme" by Heinrich Heine. That is where on a moonlit night the peasant girl Giselle, now dead, is initiated into the world of the Wilis, the eternally restless, vengeful spirits of maidens jilted by the ones they loved. Duke Albrecht, who had courted Giselle without telling her of his engagement to a princess, comes to lay flowers on her grave; Giselle had died of a broken heart when the duke's engagement was revealed. The Wilis, led by their Queen, Myrtha, try to force Albrecht to dance to death, as they do other men, but the power of Giselle's love saves him by enabling him to dance until daybreak when the magic of the Wilis disappears.

Similarly, the tanka poet Ishii Tatsuhiko, who, as we've seen, defines yūgen as "artistically contrived ambiguity," cites two examples of yūgen in music: Gustav Mahler's *Das Lied von der Erde* (*The Song of the Earth*), a Symphony for tenor, contralto (or baritone), and orchestra, with German translations of classical Chinese poems for lyrics, and Takemitsu Tōru's *November Steps*, which is for biwa, shakuhachi, and orchestra, a piece commissioned by the New York Philharmonic.

But, when it comes to literature, "*The Tale of Genji* is yūgen," Ishii says, adding, à la Harold Bloom, "In Japan for the last thousand years, true art has been that which attained the state of yūgen, which is to say an attempt to approach the world of *The Tale of Genji*."

Now, when the twentieth century was about to come to a close, amazing news hit Japan—amazing if only to those well versed in the eleventh-century romance: the Ministry of Finance announced that it had chosen a scene in the "Suzumushi" chapter of the *Tale of Genji Pictorial Scroll* for the design on the back of a special ¥2,000 bill to commemorate the Group of Eight Okinawa Summit, in the summer of 2000. How was the news amazing?

The 2000-yen Bill

"Suzumushi" describes mainly Genji fussing about Onna Sannomiya. On the night of the fifteenth of Eight Month one year, he visits her. In the sea of tinkling, shirring insects, Onna Sannomiya, once his wife, now a nun, takes a moment from her prayers to observe, in a poem, that, even though the autumn is painful to her, she cannot shake off her attachments to the voices of *suzumushi*. Lexicographers tell us that the *suzumushi*, "bell insect," here is the old name of what is today called *matsumushi*, "pine insect," *Xenogryllus marmoratus*, whereas the *matsumushi* was called *suzumushi*, *Homoeogryllus japonicus*. The distinction matters: "pine insects" make somewhat high-pitched, but short, delicate sounds, while "bell insects" make sounds that are as high-pitched and delicate but of longer duration.

That same night, while Genji is visiting Onna Sannomiya, Retired Emperor Reizei's invitation to come to his abode arrives. Genji responds, and the two spend some time composing poetry.

Now, as we have seen, Genji has affairs with many women. Among them is Fujitsubo, the second wife of Genji's father, Emperor Kiritsubo, who is said to have an unreal resemblance to Genji's mother who died after giving birth to him. The result of this illicit liaison is Reizei. But he was officially born the emperor's tenth son, hence Genji's younger brother. It was a pictorial depiction of this meeting between the two princes, Genji and Reizei—officially two brothers, but in truth, father and son—that the Finance Ministry chose for the ¥2,000 bill.

The decision of the Ministry—the most august government body!—to use this scene for a monetary design created a fascinated disbelief among those in the know. As Ishii put it, "Does this mean that a secret a thousand years old is now officially sanctioned?"

The move prompted Ishii—who regards the "Suzumushi" chapter as most yūgen in the tale that embodies yūgen—to compose a sequence of tanka. So, we may conclude our inquiry into yūgen with his sequence. It is entitled *Otōto no chichi* (*Younger Brother's Father*).

'Tis thee, my self, that for myself I praise,
Painting my age with beauty of thy days.
　　　　　　　　—Shakespeare, *Sonnet* 62

闇雲に鈴虫すだく。弟を(父さながらに)愛した男
Blindly bell insects tintinnabulate. The man who
　　loved his younger brother (as father would)

だつてさあ！　魂に疵(癒しがたく)あればこそそのたち
　　ゐのみやび
Well, you know! Because his soul's wounded
　　(incurably) he comports himself elegantly

「おとこみこ生まれたまひぬ」との報せ、ありし日、人の
　　生は秋となり——
The news was, "A prince was born," a day in the
　　past, his life's grown autumnal——

母を恋ふる子は母ゆゑに子を生す、と　....すくなくも
　　心に生す、といふ
A son in love with mother makes her bear a child
　　because she's mother, ... at least in his
　　heart, they say

父の子はわが子・わが子は他人の子、で、慈悲深き先
　　帝は罪の子
Father's son is mine · mine is someone else's, so,
　　the compassionate former emperor is sin's son

「罪といふもの時を経ていよよ美し」といふ、その錯誤
　　美し
"What's called sin becomes more beautiful as
　　time passes," they say, that fallacy　beautiful

むかしむすべるちぎり、とぞ！　新しき紙幣もてつぐのふ
　　べき明日
Love made once, right!　A new bank note with
　　which to atone for it tomorrow

罅割るる逢瀬の記憶。実母に似し継母とは、実は、(実
　　母かもしれぬ)
Cracked memory of trysts. Stepmother resem-
　　bling mother, in fact, (may be mother)

のがるべき何の宿世かひたすらにふけぬる空おもしろ
　　き御遊に
What fate to escape from single-mindedly deepen-
　　ing sky fascinating an imperial visit

弟，と子を呼ぶ不実。ふけゆけば（継）母のごと秋はな
　つかし

Iniquity of calling younger brother son. Night
　deepening like (step)mother autumn is close

はなやかにをかし。（母待つ）松虫を鈴虫と呼ぶ（さらな
　る）不実

Gay and intriguing. The (greater) iniquity of call-
　ing pine insect (pining for mother) bell insect

みづからを恃む男、とみづからを蔑すれば．．．．　　月や
　＞さしあがる

This a fellow who's reliant on himself, he despises
　himself as such. . . .　　The moon rises a bit

覗き込む鏡？　否とよ弟と兄とは今宵、異ものならず

Peering into a mirror? No sir younger brother
　and older brother tonight, no different

おそろしと思ひしことの報い、か、と、ふと思ふ。今（！）
　絶えし虫の音

Retribution for what I thought horrible, is, it,　I
　wonder. Now (!) insects' sounds stop

かさねあふ（それぞれの）罪ゆゑに（さらに）美しき物
　語、を、閉ぢ、む。

Because of the sins (of each one) that overlay the
　story's (more) beautiful, as, I, close, it.

HIROAKI SATO, who was born in Taipei, in 1942, has published three dozen translations into English of Japanese poems, classical and modern, mostly selections of individual poets. Among them, *From the Country of Eight Islands: An Anthology of Japanese Poetry* (Doubleday, 1981), with Burton Watson, won the PEN American Center translation prize; *Breeze Through Bamboo: Kanshi of Ema Saikō* (Columbia University Press, 1997) the Japan-U.S. Friendship Commission translation prize; and his work with his wife Nancy, *So Happy to See Cherry Blossoms* (Red Moon Press, 2014), the Kyoko Selden Memorial Translation Prize. *So Happy* is an annotated translation of a selection from the haiku poet Mayuzumi Madoka's anthology of haiku by survivors of the 2011 tsunami, earthquake, and nuclear reactor meltdowns.

Sato writes a monthly column for *The Japan Times*, "The View from New York."